PEPPER SEED

This book is dedicated to
Clara Charles Booker and Rita Charles.

MALIKA BOOKER

PEPPER SEED

PEEPAL TREE

ACKNOWLEDGEMENTS

My thanks go out to the editors of the following publications in whose pages some of these poems (or versions of them) have appeared: *Atlas, Cave Canem Anthology xii; poems 2010-2011, Ether Books, Generations, Long Poem Magazine, Poetry from Art (Tate Modern), Rain of Poems Anthology, London 2013, Red: Contemporary Black British Poetry (Peepal Tree), St Somewhere, Ten New Poets (Bloodaxe), Transition, Vinyl 8.*

I am very grateful to Moniza Alvi, Kwame Dawes, Toi Dericotte, Maura Dooley, Nick Drake, Cornelius Eady, Thomas Sayer Elis, Bernardine Evaristo, Terrance Hayes, W.N. Herbert, Angela Jackson, Mimi Khalvati, Daljit Nagra, Pascale Petit, Carl Phillips, Claudia Rankine, Jo Shapcott, Francis Spufford, Nathalie Teitler and Natasha Trethewey, for all of their advice, encouragement and mentorship over the years

Special thanks to my creative community: Bobby Baker, Jan Blake, Ruth Borthwick, Geraldine Collinge, Philip Cowen, Sarah Ellis, Anthony Joseph, Peter Khan, Nick Makoha, Rachel Mars, Lisa Mead, Deirdre Osborne, Nii Ayikwei Parkes, Roger Robinson, Jacob Sam La Rose, Dorothea Smartt, Imani Wilson and Karen McCarthy Woolf for all of their support and love over the years.

I would like to also thank organisations and groups like: Apples and Snakes, The Arvon foundation, The British Council, Spread the Word, The Poetry School, The Advanced Seminar group at the Poetry School, My Cave Canem Workshop family, The Complete Works family, and Malika's Kitchen, on whose courses some of these poems were initially written.

I am indebted to my close family and friends for all of their continued love and encouragement: Suzanne Alleyne, Abena Bambeje, Margaret Bambeje, Clara Charles Booker, Kwesi Booker, Philip Booker, Randolph Boyce, Iteah Charles, Natasha Charles, Rita Charles, Udean Charles, Kayo Chingonyi, Isele Cooper, Nicola Griffiths, Rudriene Hall, Fitzgerald Honger, Sharon Modeste, Dean Ricketts, Morris Roots and Karen Sobers through out my writing career.

I would like to express my sincerest gratitude to Arts Council England who awarded me with a Time to Write Grant. My Producers at PeopleBrandsEvents for their tireless support and advocacy.

I would also like to acknowledge that this book was partially written in Kočevje, Slovenia with support of The Center for Slovenian Literature, Public agency for Cultural Activities and Cultural Society Badger and Partners.

I am also deeply appreciative of the close reading and untiring support of my editors Kwame Dawes and Jeremy Poynting as well as all of the staff at Peepal Tree for their wonderful support.

CONTENTS

4: *Altars*

5: *Epilogue*

1: TESTAMENT

We are women who ban our bellies with stripes from the full moon... we buried our hope too long... we are rooting at the burying spot, we are uncovering our hope... — Lorna Goodison, "We Are the Women"

GRANNY'S LOVE POEMS

Imagine her different, a fairy-tale granny
cooking fudge for brown cinnamon girls like me.
Her pale sugar eyes twinkle.

Imagine a Guyanese bush woman
boiling root teas to punch out my fever,
her tough palms gentling my brow,
her smile stretching me,
this child, this budding sun flower.

The truth is not a love poem.
How can I talk about my granny?
Red skin, pretty yet brutal,
her aftertaste a bitter root.

RED ANTS BITE

1

You will be a whore just like your mother
Granny told me all the time,
like saying good morning.

I tried to make her love me,
but her mouth was brutal,
like hard-wire brush, it scraped me,

took skin off my bones, made me bleed
where no one could see,
so I'd shrink, a tiny rocking foetus.

You will end up on your back, scunt spread out
feet sprawl out, whoring. Who tells a child that?
Yet I loved her. She was my granny,

and I wanted her to love me back,
but everyday her words
put this hard thing deep inside me.

2

I wanted her to give me juicy mangoes and kisses,
I wanted pepperpot and tennis rolls;
she gave me rocks and hard stone,

pelted me each day, and I loved her still.
I told my doll that too much coconut oil
in Granny's hair rancid her mouth.

I am grown and the smell of mothballs
curdles my stomach. I wanted mangoes and kisses:
You will be a whore just like your mother.

My father was her everything,
my brother her world.
Her daughters reaped zigar.

3

Her mouth spat, *You black ugly scunt.*
I was her black thick molasses, dunce and sour,
her burnt cassava. I was pone charred in the oven,
I was strong bitters, a brew better off unborn.

And I still wished her eyes could swallow me whole
the way they did my brother Philip. He would hug me
to transfer Granny's glow to my world and I love him still.
Even when baby Kwesi came along, she never let go
of her apple-eye, but he never let go of us.

4

Yes! You red-skin, mixed-blood, nigger woman,
young, you were gold in Guyana's sun,
your face a dark cream to my bitter chocolate,
eyes hazel like mine. We are kin, you and I.
Your blood pumps through me. How could you
scratch me so deep, leaving lacerations?

Yes, Jesse, tell me what hardened your heart
to your son's first-born girl-child? Tell me,
Granny, now you dead, buried
in that Buxton graveyard, do you cuss me still?

Remember when Mummy went away
you came to stay at our house;
I was your shadow, how I followed you
wanting to fix the wrong you saw in me.
Your cruel tongue banished me to slide down
my wall in the corner crying, *Oh meh Goy, why?*
Granny, what I do to you, eh?

5

It was the house over by the Buxton train line,
the house with the wooden front steps
and the old white rocking chair, those stairs
where you followed Mum, heaping curses
like red ants' bites, spewing *Rasshole, scunt, whore.*

Your son had outside women? So what!
Mum ran ashamed; necks craned windows
as you peppered her skin with cuss,
till she flogged a taxi on the highway.

Years later Mum tells me the story
after I ask her to go back to Guyana with me.
The entire plane journey Mum mutters, *Wicked woman.*
We walk up those same wooden stairs,
the divorced wife, the scarred granddaughter.

At ninety-six you could claim fifty years,
that day I saw you sit in the rocking chair,
saw my mother part your hair, pour coconut oil,
massage, then plait, her fingers caressing strands.

It's water under the bridge, she tells me later.
I can't talk past the words buried deep,
can't talk past the men I froze beneath,

your words branded under the skin
inside my thighs, legs spread like a whore.

Oh mother, humbled I watch you
plait the hair of an old woman
I wanted to love me years ago.

6

Jesus look where you brought me from,
I was down in the world doing what I please
But look where you bought me from...

He had me one and let me go,
I don't know why Satan let me go...
Caribbean Gospel – Jump for Jesus.

I lived till me turn one hundred and one,
live through back-break in backra sun.
I was a slave baby mixed with plantation white.
This creamy skin draw buckman, blackman,

coolieman, like prize. And if you did hear sweet talk,
if you did see how much fine fuck I get.
Is hard life, hard, hard life and only one son I bear.
My mother tell me to kill di girl child dem –

they only bring hard ears. *Jessie, harden you heart*
to them girl. But I tell you, Miss, I never kill no child,
and is one boychild I breed, only one, then pure girls.
I didn't right to vex?

I was the lone woman every man want to advantage,
I had was to sharpen meh mouth like razor blade,

turn red in seconds till bad word spill blood.
Scunt-hole child, you want sorry?

Jessie Spenser never tell a soul sorry when she live,
you sure not getting one now me dead.
Wait for that and you go turn dust.
And what I ever do you, Missy?

I ever fire licks like rain scatter on ground
in rainy season pon you skin? No.
I tell you nuff ole higue story on back stairs.
I toughen you soffie-ness, mek man can't fuck you
easy so. So fuck off, leave the dead some peace.

PEPPER SAUCE

I pray for that grandmother, grinding her teeth,
one hand pushing in fresh hot peppers, seeds and all, turning
the handle of that old iron mill, squeezing the limes, knowing
      they will burn and cut raw like acid.
She pours in vinegar and gets Anne to chop five onions
      with a whole bulb of garlic,
      Chop them up real fine girl, you hear?
And Anne dicing, and crying, relieved that no belt has blistered her skin,
      no knife handle smashed down onto her knuckles
until they bleed for stealing money from she grandmother purse.

I hear she made Anne pour in the oil and vinegar
      and stir up that hot sauce, how she hold her down.
I hear she tied that girl to the bedposts,
      strung her out naked, like she there lying on a crucifix.
I hear she spread she out, then say,
      I go teach you to go and steal from me, Miss Lady.
I hear she scoop that pepper sauce out of a white enamel bowl,
      and pack it deep into she granddaughter's pussy,
I hear there was one piece of screaming in the house that day.
      Anne bawl till she turn hoarse,
         bawl till the hair on the neighbours skin raise up,
         bawl till she start hiss through her teeth,
         bawl till she mouth could make no more sound,
I hear how she turn raw,
how that grandmother leave her there all day,

I hear how she couldn't walk or talk for weeks.

DEATH OF AN OVERSEER
(c1815 –1817)

1

The overseer dead and he whip sprout
scarlet lilies. Whole cane fields bowed
and weeds run riot,
mosquitoes stop suck blood
and fireflies lose their light.
Yea, he who wield whip with skill, dead;
he who hit them roped bodies wearing blindfold,
he who lash don't miss, dead.

He who sing, *This job is too sweet,* as he fleck,
bloody raindrops from blistering skin, gone,
causing women to raise up they red petticoats
and dance, trampling he grave,
while machetes pound stone, lips drown rum,
and burn on highwine.

2

He disappeared from their thoughts
in a finger click. There was one-piece of no funeral
where Angie wrap that long skirt tight
so she could sway to leaves clapping
on the trees where she used to hang and swing,
licks raining on her skin
making marks like scattered rice.
Oh the splek and splak of that rope!

Now she prays to God to pelt him
with hard rock, to peel he skin
from he bones, make he crawl like swine,
this day when the mosquitoes strike
and the fireflies cease to glow.

3

Who beat drum and chant themselves into trance?
Who plant flower seed with light heart? Who talk
to jumbie, begging them to whip he hard down there,
beat he with bamboo, make he body bear red hibiscus,
he face turn ripe tomato, make he seed dry and burn?

Oh now he dead, life sweet like ripe sugar cane
and children's laughter fresh like spring water.

MINETTA SPEAKS

(Bocage Estate, St Marks, Grenada, 1812)

> *I am only human, yes I am just a woman,...*
> *show me the stairway I have to climb,*
> *Lord for my sake teach me to take one day at a time.*
> After Christy Lane's song "One Day at a Time".

1

Some days rage mek me spit and claw,
those days I fling words like hard stone,
kiss teeth, then scratch-up the man back.

Other days I lie here eyes squeezed,
a crushed hibiscus, petals ripped,
his hard green banana juking my saltfish,

my pat-a-cake just an open wound
to poke till it bruise up. I lie real still
and stiff, hands clenched, toes curled – inside is war.

Then I fly away, leave my body
like free bird. Like God. In that hot sky,
watch his naked pale backside pump;

see how my face cringe up, mouth hissing
like ah sipping hot tea. Afterwards I walk
feet spread out; everything bruised.

2

Abraham carry he son to sacrifice,
but God come in time, save he from sharp knife.
God don't save me. He hawk-eying babies
slipping my womb too soon,
born dead, buried in the garden patch.
He don't come when I squeeze cloth
over my baby girl face till it quiet,
save for mosquito and crapaud noise.
God don't come when I dash way pregnant belly
with bush tea. No, he don't come when I grind
glass with mortar pestle to mix
in Master's baby's food, muttering,
What sweet in goat mouth
go sour in he bam bam.

3

Big belly, I stoop and bend in
a sea of dancing sugar cane,

like a dirty stain on white cloth
no bleach can clean. My dreams are simple:

Please some food, no lash, a little rest
to ease backache and vomit,

when spit force up mi mouth
as baby cause bad feelings, begging God,

Please let this one don't sell,
eyes wanting to bus hard rain, blinking fast

before something breaks and cracks
like egg shell. But I harden my heart

like tough goat, bend and swing my cutlass,
sweat soaking my clothes.

As I clap, I hum, *There is power in the blood,*
power in the blood; hum and chop all day.

4

Singing, *I'll fly away home*, them elders took flight,
gone just so. Flocks of runaway slaves flew back
to Africa, dressed in calico like angels.
They left armed only with starched backs and faith,
guided by starlight, singing all the way back home.
Old people used to say, *We are earth's salt, let none*
pass your lips; say, *Put salt in bird tail to ground he,*
make he can't fly, make he easy to catch. Hard ears,
we kissed our teeth, ate salt beef. Now we can't fly
home in white by dark night. We foot stick to earth
like Lot's wife. Now runaways are dog bait,
hunted and fetched back, so we dream of death
when we spirit will fly to glory as the living sing in grief,
One fine morning when my life is over I'll fly away home.

BRIXTON MARKET

I would stand at market stalls
and watch her take days to pick,
how she would test the okra,
bending their tips, placing only
the ones that snapped into a brown paper bag;
the way she scrutinised the yam,
feeling and weighing it in her palm;
plantains picked one by one
like an artist selecting her tools.
Flawed produce would be haggled
to the last, and sometimes
she would turn her back and walk
to make her point and get her way.
I pulled that shopping trolley
into the stench of meat shops,
waiting as she pointed to red slabs
she wanted. How many times
would she point and weigh
to change her mind!
I would stare at the goose-bumped
boiling chicken hanging from ceiling,
the cow-foot, and severed pig tails.
I tried to hold my breath at the fish stall
as she chose the kippers, and we waited
for the snapper to be cleaned.
At Kwik Save, each can of baked beans
was vetted for dents, each egg
delicately lifted, searched for cracks.
I would learn that this is how my grandmother
taught her, kneeling in the bush uprooting dasheen
on the family land. She, too, hawk-eyed,
tested each provision to know
what was ripe, ready and good to cook.

NOTTING HILL

Those old hips shake your pleated skirt today, aunty.
You are no church girl. All day you jamming
behind big truck, laughing, bottom rolling for so,
feet chipping, skirt swaying as if for its blasted self.

You are no church girl. No bells ring in the sermon,
no bible in you hand. No, the sermon is Kaiso music
and it sweet too bad, pitching out of speaker stacks
or sticks licking steel pan with a tin ti tin tin.

You are no church girl, as your feet trample tar roads,
belting out lyrics: *Audrey, where you get that sugar,*
darling, there is nothing sweeter, feting out winter blues,
like this music is a Pentecostal preacher and you body
testifying, like Baptist rhythm hold on pon you.

You were no church girl when that body fetched water
from standpipe in St David Street, bucket balanced on head,
hip undulating, humming kaiso, or you slipped through back room
windows to party in moonlight with fresh-faced boys,
dancing to Calypso Rose, Kitchener and Sparrow.

You are no church girl, yet no rum or strong spirit touch
your lips as your feet pelt hard slaps on pavement stone.
And is how much policeman you pinpoint, target
and jump on, bottom rolling back on black uniform.

Today you eyes freeze them fresh-faced boys
trying to move in slyly on me, you niece,
Move, leave she lone, she too young, that child not ready,
them eyes say, then you hug me up and wine.

2: CRUCIAL TIMES

We are part of an old story and involved in it are migrations of winds, of ocean currents, of seeds, songs, and generations of nations
  — Joy Harjo, "The Psychology of Earth and Sky"

I am trodding these roads of trials and tribulations, I've seen where some have died in desperation to keep battling down sentence, fighting against conviction...
  — Bunny Wailer, "Fighting Against Conviction"

SAUTEURS

I stand at this cliff's edge; water froths below;
the tar road behind disappears. I see only down.
The sun dips; perspiration rolls down my back.
Here men kissed babies, then flung them out,
like skimming stones over the water,
hurled children like sacks.
Elders shuffled to the edge, then said,
Push us, we ready. Young men stood,
spread their hands and dived,
brown flocks in flight, migrating.

So they began to rename.
Grenada: *that is not our name*
Caribs: *that is not our name*
Grenadian Dove Leptotila: *that is not our name*
Hook-billed Kite: *that is not our name*
Hummingbird: *that is not our name*
Oh soured baptism.

I stand at the cliff's edge
where US fighter planes roared
and men ran from the noises of hell,
bullets finding victims like darts find board.
Them jets hit worst than hurricane Janet.
Men dive for cover, girl, and who pee they pants,
who jump off cliff and dead, just so dry, dodging
bullets. Mango, cocoa, banana, and palm trees
danced to them bullet drums, bending backwards,
spine cracking, splintering, them trees lashing and carrying on
like they dancing for the devil, and the way
de damn jets screech make grown men cry.

And so they began to rename.
Rebels: *that is not our name*
Communist: *that is not our name*
Military coup: *that is not our name*
Cuban headquarters: *that is not our name*
Oh soured baptism.

I stand at this cliff's edge waiting for the bones
to rise and reclaim their names.

SESTINA FOR GRENADA

You can drive around the entire island
in one day. A place where lush fauna and young girls
flourish, sticks beat steel pan and a woman's waters
break each minute, sunshine sprawls heat
onto curvy cliff roads till rainy season
slings in to breed trees heavy with fruit.

Here schoolgirls' bodies ripen like fruit
to be plucked by grown men lusting for island
hips to stake in dark pastures and season
with sperm till their breasts swell. Naive girls
unable to block nutmeg babies from men on heat,
who long to swim in all kind of fresh water;

men harvesting kids destined to cross the water
for foreign. No one left to plant cocoa, so fruit
rots into the soil. MTV youths, who can't take the heat
and scorn the bruising coarseness of island
farming, flock towards Uncle Sam for girls
to marry for green card, or overstay their season.

Cricket is replaced by New York Knicks' season
tickets; youths yearn for home and sea-water,
squashed into housing projects, little girls
five to a bed, like bunched bananas. Force-ripe fruit
begins to lose flavour in crack city's hustle. Island
ways fade, staying warm means raising the heat

so roaches swarm parquet floors. Calls home create heat
for barrels crammed with brand names to season
the local EC dollar, stretch it further. *Oh spice island,
what we leave you for? We miss your fresh river water.
Life here is sweet, but sickly, too, like rotten fruit.*
Yet they go back to pose and boast up: flash US girls,

27

build big house, spinning good-life yarns for girls
they left behind; singing success hymns of salvation to heat
up the blood. So dreams obscure the local fruit
from pregnant trees, rotting in the grass. And rainy season
raise a drought of farmers, making people buss eye-water
scraping money to buy the produce of this fertile island.

No one left on this island to plant yam and dig dirt in the heat
on family plots green with bush. No hands season the land
with water. Only a cycle of young girls endlessly bearing fruit.

LAMENT FOR THE ASSASSINATION
OF COMRADE WALTER RODNEY
June 23rd 1980

1: The News

The home was cold;
a mother, brother, sister sat empty,
guts screwed with news that their father dead.

They say he body parts scatter all across Bent street,
they say like Seth scatter Osiris across black tar.

2: Procession

That day a donkey cart tote his coffin
to the graveside. There was curfew,
but who hitched lift, who walked in hot sun,
who jumped into hire-taxi or old bus,
whipped donkey, or drove car,
through tears and sweat in backra sun?

3: Prayer

They say how crows cover the place like plague,
when the bomb blow up that poor man car.

Oh they father dead, leave them to their grief,
their Kingdom ruined, their world forever marred,
as knees are bent under this heavy weight.

Oh they father dead, may he rest in peace.
Each time, they remember the car, burnt, charred,
they know their father won the last debate.

4: Salute

If you did see people! Police, guns cocked
and ready to fire, had to stand back
as swelling footsteps cracked the highroads.
That day poets strangled words and the world wept.
That night placards cuff down politicians,
chanting:

Who will speak for us now?
Who will raise up the corrupt skirts of the rich
and show us their dirty panties?
That night his bones tossed and turned in the coffin.
That night there was no moon. There was no moon.

5: His Wife

His wife became a cactus
that day she dragged her body
across the cut grass.

It was the arch of the words
"husband, dead, bomb".
That day her bridge collapsed,

wooden planks hurled
towards the violent water
churning in the drop below.

GUYANA

You live in ruins. Your dollar value has decreased.
Your children leave you before they can wipe
childhood from their eyes. El Dorado fuels
the throats of grown men nightly in rum shops,
liming to drown out hard life and rancid dreams.
El Dorado takes off the edge in this place
where life rough like gnarled tree bark.

O Guyana, your sins are soggy mud, bright brown
in the firelight burn of the sun. O Guyana, some days
gold teeth laugh under banana sun, some days
banana skin get sick with big muddy spots,
like dark tree bark, like brown sour mud,
like amber El Dorado rum. I want to pour
that rum on the floor for your wounded spirits.
I want to pour El Dorado for the departed.

ISLAND GRIEF AFTER HURRICANE IVAN.

All over the island is pure bacchanal.
      Zinc roofs dance feral in the pitch dark
and all man jack gone wild. Everything
      back in front. Crapaud smoke he pipe

tonight as shack shack trees shoo shoo
      with mammy apple trees, whilst Jumbie
Umbrella macco the scene. Everywhere
      is pure jab jab mass, a fierce sound clash

driving all the mongoose to run in circles
      like they catch gigga. The rain fall zig
zags like fat flies, raising choirs of mosquitoes
      from rivers, humming black clouds, infectious.

Yet sugarcane stalks refuse to sway
      just stand like rigid salutes. Bay Leaf
and Cinnamon stop making joke
      and start to pray hard until Breeze drag

off her clothes and bawl for Moonlight
      to sing a lullaby, sing on and on
till her voice grows hoarse. Then Bitter Aloes
      start fighting with Black Sage bush,

throwing hard cuff as dropping coconuts
      thump voop vap, and it is madness
in the river-water where tiny titiree
      swirl and bubble. Meanwhile Manicou

and Jack Fish lament Nutmeg's demise
      as bazoodee island parrots stand numb
like statues, their claws curled
      around branches of pommerac trees.

Moonlight is paged to cradle the moaning
        wounded. Oh Spice Isle, let it not die here.
Oh Lord, there is pepper in the deads'
        mouths and coffins fly overhead.

SALTFISH

My mother wanted to boil the salt out of the fish,
so much harsh salt, then chip that saltfish smaller
and smaller, so she could cope with the hawked spit
of her patients, their hatred gutting her raw
so that some days she wanted to tell them,
It's only skin, we bleed the same underneath,
but she held it in. Some days she wanted to crawl
back into her mother's belly, her little island home
and be safe. Some days she wished she had stayed
in that small place because if you study the damn dogs
in this place, they go bite you up, break you down.
Everyday you feel like your teeth cracking on hard
stale cassava bread. This place ain't winning at all;
is like they don't realise we can still go back home.

HEATHROW AIRPORT IMMIGRATION 2007

When she hear say alla dem haffi go back,
Charlene start feel like dark night.

She drop so much style pon she friend dem back a yard,
now dem a go laugh afta her.

It bruk her heart fi see di two pickney dem a hug up,
ah look like poor ting inna di corna,

yet it never sink in till she start see people beg and sob,
fi her stomach drop till it meet her big toe,

mek her fall braps pon concrete floor and bawl.
One smart-dress ooman start hiss inna posh voice,

Get up, get up, have you no shame?
If she never feel so bad she woulda box her down.

One pleat-skirt granny, pull her up, tell her
fe stop cry, *Tru, God knows best*.

How she did want to spit in God's eye that day!
Wha God know bout shame and sacrifice?

Lord Gad, all di money spend pon visa gone,
dem nah even gi her back di flight money.

EXODUS

She does not talk about that time.
She has buried it deep in the earth
where you bury shit. She chucked it
into a dark hole then shovelled dirt
on top. Buried it with no wake,
no funeral, no coffin, no fanfare,
buried it whilst it was raw, stink and bitter.

It was early September. The phone ring.
Jerk out of sleep. Fumble. The red sky
of pre-dawn through my bare window.
My cousin's Guyanese tones, low,
whispering, voice broken. She sobs,
till I, too, begin to cry.

She stutters, stops, starts, tells me
about an advert, a plane ride.
They promised her work and a US visa.
I am a prisoner somewhere
in the South; they take my passport,
work us long hours, deduct our pay
for food and board, then give us a trickle.
I made more back home. We pick fruit all day.

She left her girlchild home in her mother's care,
now can't send them no money.
I can't see me way… help me, she sobs.
I make phone calls to older aunts in New York,
not new to this, who tell me they will take care of it.
A month later they call to say, *We have her.*
How? I ask. But they have buried it, too.
We do not talk about them things.

ILLEGAL IMMIGRANT
after *The Coral Reef* by Mike Nelson

You are a coarse crocus bag, a downtrodden rice sack,
your silence scrapes a painful music.

The clocks have stopped for you and when I will them to work
the minutes crawl the way dust gathers on its victims.

3: LAMENTATIONS

I am making use of the one thing I learned of all the things my father tried to teach me: the art of memory.
— Li Young Lee "This Room and Everything in It"

and that was just lamentations
and that was just lamentations
it was not history
— Derek Walcott, "The Sea is History"

WARNING

1

Some great grandmother told her daughter,
Never let no man hit you and sleep,
pepper the food, boil hot water and throw,
use knife and make clean cut down there,
use cutlass and chop, then go police.
Each daughter told over and over,
like *brush your teeth*, till it stick.
How my mother run-way man with cutlass,
chase him. How my gran use cutlass pon table
to explain to her man, *Don't lose your blasted mind*
and raise that hand on me.
And so we are shaped, moulded and made hard.
I remember my aunt kicked her man out
after her child was born, cut him dead
like rotten wood, after he use her like boxing bag,
kicking her womb as she lay on the floor.
That day her blood boiled through swell eye
and buss skin. She knew he could not sleep; he knew
she wanted to kill him bad bad, chop him dead…

2

Raised in London soil and Guyana sun,
I never understood that need for cutlass,
where it came from, till I visited Grenada,
a place where man fist pound woman flesh
like kneading hard dough. I see bull strength
knock girls flat out when she man full of rum
and carnival. How Ronald buss lash in he woman ass
every Friday and Saturday night, kick she down,
buss she tail. And next day is black eye and bruise.

As Pauline clings onto Ronald's foot, saying
she love him through each blow, I understand.

3

I never knew I had it. Thought I was soft,
till that night my friend could not drive
and I offered him my bed to sleep.
I felt something in his look, he and I
alone in that room, and my blood raised up.
My pores swelled, I went to the kitchen,
took down that knife, marched upstairs,
told him, *I cutting it off if you lose your mind.*
Don't think it and if you do, don't sleep.

PRAYER

My mother tells me, *Your womb*
will dry and shrivel up.
I dance through life, deaf,
no child planned in my party.

Age's aches slow her, she prays
for *Grandma* on a child's lips.

She wants to touch her future

but each year

there is no baby.

ARRIVAL

When I saw your father, before your birth,
I saw a boulder, its broad chest teetering

on a slope, awkward as his skin stretched
and cracked, losing its old self.

I saw him weigh each decision carefully,
his life mission sharpened like a pencil.

I saw him testing *father* on his tongue, rolling it
in his mouth like hot liquid and squinting at its burn.

As you stretched your mother's belly,
so he stretched. He shed parts to prepare.

I saw a man naked and unsure, rolling *daddy*
around his tongue, preparing like a raw trumpeter

stretching abstract notes, creating jazz.
I saw you make him a man.

CEMENT

Last week my tears were sucked out
with our aborted child. Yesterday
in the shower, pain contorted me,
I squatted, expelled a souvenir:

red, liver-textured, squeezed out.
I scooped it up and flushed it away.
You were not there. Your absence
no longer makes me cry.

My tears are gone, so I plaster my heart
against every grit-worried wound.
Now I understand older black women
like my aunts, their hard posture,

why I never saw them cry.
My father made my mother stony,
a martyr for her kids, brittle and bitter,
till my stepdad unbricked her wall;

layer by layer I watched it crumble.
My aunt, shattered by fists, blocked her heart;
stone cold, her tears dried up.
All my life, I never saw her cry, until foetal

in a hospital bed, wrapped in my mother's arms,
facing death, tears tracking her face,
she whispered, *I am scared*.
Crying for all her tear-barren years.

Washing water-diluted blood down the drain,
bleaching the bath tiles white, I want to bawl
my eyes out, but I have learnt my lesson well.
Each passing day hardens my voice.

ERASURE

This is no elegy; no one can write elegies
for such as you. There are no scuff marks here
for your erasure. No etches on a strong barked tree.

There was no grief. You are my silence.
Why do you choose to rise now like shifting sand
blown by a slight breeze?

You were my simple crime against humanity,
and, like a criminal, I claim no regrets.
I buried you too deep to call you a name;

you are my trail of invisible lines
like the stretch marks that did not have time to form.
No guilt resides in my house.

I did what we women have always done.
I froze the tears into a block of ice
buried so deep that the guilt is a cold in me,

a thing that will not melt.
What can I say to you who never breathed, you callous dust?
I can talk of sacrifices, broken lives.

I can talk of Abraham almost slashing Isaac's life.
But this was no holy decision.
I cannot tell you why I said no to you.

I am a white dress all ash and grey.
You unspeakable requiem, do not rise now.
Do not ask me the worth.

Who can measure the weight of ambition
against what could have been?

A PRAYER FOR THE DYING

Grandfather wanted to die,
his anguish at dawn, when cock crow.
He'd hear the house rise and knew he lived,
the pointer broom sweeping yet again,

his grandchildren's morning quarrels,
the scent of fresh bread
from his daughter-in-law's bakery below.
He wept all day on his hundredth birthday

in that pale blue room, under the mosquito net
in his pee-soaked bed; cried through each birthday
wish, fingers crawling faces, frail hands
replacing failed eyesight. He was a baby again.

This morning something broke, he said,
clutching that black bible. *This morning
I know is God turn he back on me,
leave me a useless burden.*

He lay in that room listening to cricket,
daily news and funeral announcements,
and we knew it hurt, all his friends buried,
his wife and mistresses long gone.

We knew it hurt past missing, past lingering,
past everything. We knew it hurt, our visits
when we sat in his room talking, hurting to see him so.
We knew and yet willed him to stay here for us.

We knew, reminded by his blue suit
hanging there, the black shoes and felt hat
he chose for his eager appointment
with the funeral parlour, twenty-five years ago.

Last night we heard his prayers.
He prayed for every one of us
then said, *Oh Lord let me come to you,*
Oh Lord, why? It is time.

WAITING FOR FATHER

Little kernels of corn explode. My mother's nose sweats,
her calm spirals into a scarlet cyclone,
those nights we popped and buttered popcorn,

then sat waiting for my father,
waiting to stick ourselves to those leather seats
in his grey Cortina, clip speakers to the windows,

and eat popcorn at the drive-in movie.
His arrival depended on the law of averages,
and statistics strongly supported non-arrival.

Evenings we sat believing it would be different.
How could he not come? He was a kite,
dancing in our clouds. How could we not see

that we clenched the fraying thread of a high flyer;
a flamboyant cockerel parading in sunshine with his floozies.
Ah Fatthaa!   How could you?   How could you?

AUTOBIOGRAPHY FOR DADDY

My blood has many relatives. They never visit.
                        — Yehuda Amichai

Your house is red wood and we do not live there.
You forsake your children just by breathing on this earth.

You walked away from brown eggshells before they hatched,
the rooster you were, strutting with your puffed-out chest.

We were skeletons lying scattered on a lawn,
green with expectation. Yet we grew in spite

of your absence, our bones brittle from malnutrition.
There is no pity left in your children for you now.

You are a stranger whose blood runs in our veins,
but blood clots.

Your children stand on the peak of that red zinc roof,
rocking, then precariously finding balance on one leg.

In the distance a bell chimes, *Close the gap*
before he dies; he is still your father.

FADED SLIPPERS

Your son lives across town with his mother.
Each nightly visit, I slip my feet
into his red Snoopy slippers,

a perfect fit, the way I want to fit
you, long to slide myself into your life.
There is no room for me here.

Our late night conversations till five am,
our bodies writhing in your cool sheets,
our arms wrapping each other in sleep,

mean nothing, except a moment to add
to strings of moments, whose names
rest in your little black book.
Women who want to stay too.

STALE

The bed sheets are tangled, my skin is sticky.
Outside night dies, dawn languidly stretches

into morning. The muggy room, heavy limbs,
lingering scent of sex convince me this is love.

Naked, I tiptoe on the icy wooden floors, search
the strewn clothes for that crotchless lace scrap

tossed in heat.
          There – behind your bed, next to my panty –

an old condom, its beige pallor your stale sticky sap.
          I glance at ours in your waste-bin.

It's gone sour.

BROTHER WARNING

Early warning

These are men who dash ripe fruit
on hard stone again and again, grind
heels on ladies' hearts, smile
into their faces like angels, climb
women's back stairs, polished

shoes breaking the treads of each stair
even when they tiptoe in. Each assault
scares me and I am their flesh and blood.
Hearts ground into red dust of hot pepper
to burn others who venture near.

Yellow warning

Your mother and I feast with your cast-out women.
After each tale we tie yellow ribbons around our tears, weep,

shame in our eyes as if we hurt them.
I want to paint yellow x's on your door

to warn the next woman of her fate;
place you in quarantine – son of my father,

my father, son of my grandfather,
my grandfather, son of my great grandfather –

be judge and executioner, mark you all yellow;
string petal necklaces to choke your neck.

Mother distributes amber to prospective
girlfriends to inform their decision making.

Red warning

It's too late; we meet them already reeled in;
slicing has begun, delicate nips. How
do you warn fish they are in danger
when they're already bleeding,
aware we are the red herrings
in the introductions?

SIN VISITS ME

They say a dead woman can't run from her coffin.
How moonshine can orchestrate nuff wild thoughts!
It's an hour past midnight and the road outside is quiet;
my thoughts are a twisting screwdriver; licks
of a dozen switches scorch my skin. Pomegranate flowers
line the road, each spread out from the other,
and their crumpled petals are the shocking red of death.
I am in the centre of this wreath. You chew chillies raw,
laugh, and spit the seeds, then tell me of the joys
of sitting on a big stone under Concord waterfall,
watching near naked boys leap off the moss-green cliffs above.
Your voice is smooth liquor. Your whirring hands speak
another language. I hold a white china cup in my hand;
funny how the cracks don't seem to show.
You in your saucy lace that binds your body like mace
covers nutmeg seeds; I am shocked by your vulgarity.
I tell you, crapaud don't have no right in salt water.
You tell me you have a right to be everywhere.

LOVE IS A REBELLIOUS BIRD
THAT NOTHING CAN TAME
after *Carmen*, Habanera

I was in love once; he flew away.
I opened the door of my cage, waited;
he never came back.
Waited at the top of a steep stair;
he would not climb;
stepped down to meet him;
he turned his back, an iron shield.
With nowhere to go, my heart
has become chipped china;
it's never been handled with care.

I was in love once
with a marauding raptor.
He flew away on the coldest night.
Last night I dreamed him. We danced
a *pas de deux* in the kitchen;
pirouettes smashed white china.
In the morning he disappeared,
rode out on a lumbering elephant.
My heart is a slashed red dress.
I want to spit pepper seeds into his eye,
but he rode away on an elephant,
a heavy bundle on his back.

I have covered my head with bhut jolokia,
lathered my soul with bird pepper.

Now I wait at the top of the stairs,
salt and black pepper sprinkled under my feet.
A lone ballerina, I dance on the grains.
My danseur is gone. Poor rejected Carmen.
L'amour est un oiseau rebelle.

PUBLIC HEALTH WARNING

Barricade your souls, ladies.
Lock up yourselves, sweet butterflies
or their pin will impale you
to the wall, make you colourful
specimens stagnant in glass cabinets.

SWEET LIQUOR

Left right, left right in the Government boots, the Government boots
I see them boots, boots, boots and more boots
On the feet of young trigger-happy recruits – The Mighty Gabby

girl, if you see thing! the way they does pile in here when fete
door bus open on saturday nights. pour in like animals. looking
sweet too bad. girl if you see the way they does parade and carry
on. how i does close meh eyes and lean back on them hard bodies
and wine. i know some of them real good. the way they move.
how they handle women bodies. the way they does roll they hip.
girl you have to know them tings, so when a man come jam
behind you, you could know if is friend or foe without turning
round and looking up in he face. or in case the place too dark to
make out they face. you know if to walk off or stay there. girl, i
know they faces real good but never look in they eyes.

if you does see the way they hold on to rum bottles like is com-
munion. like is holy. like is they saviour. the way they does crawl
all up inside hard liquor. girl, if you see them wring out johnny
walker bottle. squeeze every drop. knock back wray and nephew
just like real beast riding they soul.

girl, to see sweet young ting hurt so bad does make pain buss meh
belly. when they play that destra song that say, *everybody everybody*
bounce somebody, bounce somebody, girl, if you see ting! a host of
unruly joy. them man does tek over the dancefloor and smash
they bodies, flesh hitting flesh, jumping and hollering like the
army evict them, like them bodies have nuff sin to wuk out they
system. last night ashley tell me he name call and he going over
there soon. girl, and when he tell me dat, i mek the mistake of
looking he in he eyes. if you see them eyes! i frighten men with
eyes dead so. like all the love wring out of them. i does wonder
what the hell them see so, make sadness line they eyes like
cataract. oh lord, girl, what I see in he eyes mek meh own eye

spring water. he so young, baby still in he chin and he standing there body lean to one side, squeezing the bottle neck, choking it nah backfoot! girl, what I could say eh! stupid tie up meh tongue, so I jus do hold onto him all night, sweet he up with meh body, and pile he ass with more liquor.

AFTER LIMING IN THE LOCAL RUM SHOP
ON DIAMOND STREET,

he slashed his cutlass across her face,
her raised hand failed to shield

against the second blow.
One finger cut clean off.

She deserved it, Auntie Julie said.
I know, if it was her daughter,

she would hunt and gut him
like wild manicou.

Reggae blares from Eggie's rum shop,
Miss Junes practices hymns for the church choir.

This street is a child's playground
where all the sounds battle until they harmonise.

But there's no fight here. Well,
two little girls punch up, stop talk, then make up.

They say *Is not he fault, too much Clarke's Court
full he belly and heat up he blood*.

She took him back in.
I hear no apology left his lips.

4: ALTARS

Once you lose someone it is never exactly
the same person who comes back
— Sharon Olds, "Feared Drowned"

VIGIL

1

Her youngest daughter searches
for a funeral dress and white veil.
Her eldest daughter folds in;
her son disappears into heroin.

I ask only that my aunt wait for me,
the way her mother waited for her,
holding death back with laboured breath,
eyes fixed ahead, living

to see her daughter that last time.
I ask her to wait so I can watch
her steady fingers turn the rosary beads,
kiss the baby hair by her ear,

smile when she tells me she is scared.
I don't want her to be alone.
I am confident, like God,
packing for my early morning flight.

At 3 am the phone rings. She's gone.
There is a still pause before I weep.

2

Today I walk along the River Thames
following a procession,
nostalgic as the season dies,

watching rust-coloured leaves litter
as Indian gods, samba dancers,
and fish lanterns glide in the night.

Last year I walked in this sea of bodies,
saying poems about crossroads
to veil-faced Orishas, lifeless puppets.

I walked dressed in white
like her face covered in that coffin.
I walked preparing for my vigil,

ticking off hours to my flight.
It's a year today.
I knew she would wait,

but she slipped out real quiet
and gone she own way.

BURIAL GROUND

There are dark places drunk with grief where water
drizzles. There are wilted flowers and dried wreaths.
There is your grave hidden back there, behind
God's back. There are clusters of Charles
buried here, neighbours in this family plot.
Two lone wooden stumps mark the grave
where you wait for that marble headstone
etched with your name. There is wild bush
and the broken fence where your nephew
crashed that rented car at your funeral,
when his vision blurred with tears. There are
the marks we leave and those that will be made.

FAITH

1

The museum is an empty house, a dead lifestyle.
In the living room, pictures of Jesus forlorn,
an old rosary hanging over the bed.
This how we lived in old days, they tell me.

I understand old ones die, like you did, Aunty,
the way your soul left your body, blank
on bleached sheets, the way these people
left their home. I look at this old bed now;
did a mother die here, choking on her spit too?
Is this her rosary? Did she lose it all?

I visit the hospital a month before you die,
your left big toe is a blackening cherry.
Cut it, we beg, but our pleas are moot;
you are Taurus. Stoic. Resolute.

That day you lost your rosary for two days,
we search under beds and in fruit bowls.
You cry nonstop all night. Nurses sift mountains
of soiled sheets until the rosary is found nestled
in your dirty pillow case. When they give it to you,
your fingers continue rolling as if it had not strayed.
Then you, who clutched your faith like a second skin,
whisper to me, *I have lost faith in my Lord.*

2

I want to write a hymn for you
where voices lift and southern Black choirs rock.

I want to write a hymn for you
where the sinners writhe, weeping bitter tears.

I want to write a hymn for you
where Baptist priests fling words at the congregation like fire
and Catholic priests throw holy water into the sky.

I want to write a classic hymn all harps and harmonicas,
a hymn where our slave grandmas lift up their long frocks
and trample the earth to sounds of tambourines.

I want to write calypso hymns, folk hymns,
reggae hymns, joyous hymns.
I want to write sweet hymns for you.

LIBATION

Slovenia 2008

It is the Night of the Dead, the graveyards are packed
as relatives lay flowers, light flames, talk to their dead.
It is beautiful: the flowers, the moon, and silence.
I am in Kocevje, my relatives buried so far away.
I do not honour anyone. I am ugly here.

How could I forsake my own dead?
Aunty, each year you placed white candles
and holy water in every doorway of our home
for our departed, then we prayed over food
left on plates with glasses of water to feed our dead.

Now no Jesus pictures hang on my wall,
No "God bless this house" sign on my door.
Yes, I write poems for you, but that is not enough;
I have forgotten our ways and am ashamed.
Are you angry that I forsake you all and our Lord?

When food falls from my mouth, I don't leave
a plate, glass and candle to light your way,
and I know, Oh Lord, I know these old ways.
Aunty, I will light candles and call all your names:
Aunty Rita, Mammy Joyce, Uncle Peter, Granny.
Yes I will call all your names.

LOSS

I remember your skinny ankles,
thin flighty hair hating to stay neat.

You loved a joke. But I don't remember
your hands, the shape of your fingers.

I remember calluses, not their location,
fingers slim like okra. But were they?

Your hands, constantly in motion
like a humming bird, dipped needles

through coarse cloth, knitted
chunky wool scarves, plaited dough

to shape bread, stitched family again
and again. Those fluttering hands are still.

Long gone your scent of coco tea,
skin more milk now than cocoa.

I ask you to show me those hands.
You stare, *Take time my child,*

you always running… Slow down.
That's no answer, I choke.

But you are gone, in your place
a butterfly. *Show me your hands…*

GRATITUDE

for no more phlegm's weight on your chest,
no more gangrene crayoning your legs
rotted black, for that day your fingers ceased
to roll the glass rosary, your lips stopped
pleading prayers to God, begging to live longer,
begging for his strength.

AUNTY RITA

White Clarke's Court is the incense at this wake;
its coarseness bruises our mouths, an unbearable
burning. Our dead ancestors lusted after you,
so they dragged you to them before your time.
Now the village dogs howl in the graveyard.

I slide one of your rosaries through my fingers.
Your death tastes the way my bone hurts after it bangs
hard against the bed edge. That rough kiss of bone and wood.
Rita, you who vetoed wood to build big concrete house,
we are gathered in your home and you, my dear, are absent.

No it wasn't lusting ancestors that craved you, just God. It was your time,
so he clasped you to him. He didn't have to drag, just sweet-talk
you, who did not want to leave your siblings, offspring,
and last grandson. The devil stood on the sidelines grinning.
His teeth looked like dog that eat wedding cake.

You gave in because all that crocheting had made you sensible.
But still *Allyuh too hardened*, so you took your own time and it was long.
Lasted till your rope of indecision finally frayed. It was then
that you greeted Madam La Diablesse with her one hoof-foot
at the crossroads, and sat down on the corner to badtalk men.

Poor Maliks raced across the globe to be at your side, but you left
too soon, now she will forever arrive too late to comfort
her ailing loves before they die. Poor headless chicken,
dragging her heavy body in the dirt, every time they tell her,
You are too late. She will have to fling herself off
Mount St Catherine's Peak just to see you alive again.

THE HOUSE ON JUBILEE STREET

The roof leaks golden brown dust,
like the sugar deadly for your diabetes.
Clean laundry is still piled on your bed.
The wardrobe shows your ageing seasons:
from flares and minis, to long pleated skirts
and silk petticoats folded neatly on the shelves.
Your bottom is indented in the cushion
of your favourite chair. A faded palm cross
hangs on the living-room wall;
tiles detach from the verandah floor;
downstairs the wood column rots.
Seven Septembers since you died,
yet no one will give the house
its last rite, and so it remains,
woodworm gnawing the roof;
everything fixed for your resurrection.

OUR LAST SUPPER

1

There are flickering tea lights on each table.
I am on stage. Suddenly there you are
in the front row, clutching your grandchild,
both of you the same age as when you died.
You are the fragile sparrow, the dull wren,
head tied in silk scarf like an old Russian peasant.
You are flounce and long-length pleated skirts
and I can see your ankles – those bird legs
still don't look able to take your weight.
You are holding the little boy in your lap.
He is Grandma's darling and you are not dead.
He clutches your hands. Here is pure love.
Each word from my rustling page meets
your little nod. You are virgin audience,
who never saw me read. I am sure this
is a dream, you sitting here so serene,
your smile saying I see you now, I see
you; and I become your preening peacock.

2

We leave the poetry event to eat.
It's that same last meal, again and again.
It's plantain slices with fresh coconut bakes.
You eat tomatoes peeled and thinly diced, I eat
spicy baked beans. You sip rich cocoa tea,

I pick out the fish bones for the baby.
I am proud of you, your voice is spring water,
bubbly and alive. We hold hands,
the baby's palms squeezed flat between ours
like a group prayer. This is red lily love.

Then a knife clatters from another table
in the empty restaurant. I wake up
and you are gone. I always want to raise
you from the dead. It is another morning,
you have gone again. I am nothing. Even
in this dream I never get to say goodbye.

SUICIDES

My room is an orange graveyard.
Ladybirds come here to die,
each day a new corpse.

They rest their polka-dot frocks
on my rotting window frame;
outside the world also dies;
black clouds drift;

trees stark, like charcoal silhouettes
spray their branches
across the horizon.

I watch them practice death
in their red funeral dresses
as dusk rapidly descends.

EPILOGUE

The women in your family have never lost touch with one another. Death is a path we take to meet on the other side... With every step you take there is an army of women watching over you.

— Edwidge Danticat, *Krik Krak*

MY MOTHER'S BLUES

My mother knows pain
a sorrowful gospel type of pain —

a slowly losing her eyesight,
eye-drops every night pain,

a headache worrying for her children overseas,
praying for their safety pain,

a stare through each night, eyes blackening,
hope they are alright pain.

Yes, my mother knows pain.

My children don't call,
do they still love me pain,

a worrysome dying grey hair black,
children too far away pain,

a will my daughter ever have children,
she is thirty-eight now pain,

a *your womb is becoming stone* sermon
for her only girl on her birthday pain.

Yes, my mother knows pain.

A what did I do wrong
bringing them up pain,

a my son has gone astray, someone put obeah on him
so I have to pray real hard pain,

a look how so-and-so children do so well,
I wish mine were like that pain.

Yes my mother knows pain.

It's the house now empty
no one to cook for pain,

and I can't let go, have to let go pain,
it's a let me tell you how to bury me pain,

I want a plain box, no fancy coffin,
or I will come back and haunt you pain,

a don't have no big set of people
coming around calling it a wake pain,

it's a let me tell you who will get what
after I am gone, so you don't fight pain,

it's a don't worry I go soon be dead and gone
and then you go miss me pain.

Yes my mother feels pain.

NOTES

"Sauteurs"

Sauteurs is the name of an area in Grenada where there is a steep hill called Leapers Hill by the French because the entire Carib nation choose to jump of the forty metre tall cliff rather than submit to the French in 1651.

On 25th October 1983, the USA invaded Grenada in Operation Urgent. It is said that people ran up to Shooters Hill for safety but were shot by the local panicked police force and that, combined with the fire from the air, caused them to jump off the cliff.

"Brother Warning"

A warning and an early warning of the same colour have the same severity, but are forecast to arrive at different times. A yellow warning means heavy rain is expected with torrential downpours and thunderstorms possible in places. The difference between a red warning and a red early warning is the lead time of the event.

Some definitions of red from factmonster.com: In Russia red means beautiful; in South Africa red is the colour of mourning; superstitious people think red frightens the devil.

ABOUT THE AUTHOR

Malika Booker is a British writer of Guyanese and Grenadian parentage. Her poems are widely published in anthologies and journals including: *Out of Bounds, Black & Asian Poets* (Bloodaxe 2012); *Ten New Poets* (Bloodaxe, 2010); *The India International Journal 2005*; and *Bittersweet: Contemporary Black Women's Poetry* (The Women's Press, 1998).

She has represented British writing internationally, both independently and with the British Council, in such countries as Slovenia, Switzerland, New Zealand, India, and Azerbaijan.

Malika Booker has also written for the stage and radio. Her one-woman show *Unplanned* toured nationwide throughout 2007. Her pamphlet *Breadfruit* was published by flippedeye in 2008, and recommended by the Poetry Book Society.

She was the first Poet in Residence at the Royal Shakespeare Company. *Pepper Seed* is her first full-length poetry collection.